STRAIGHTFORWARD LEADERSHIP AND MANAGEMENT STRATEGIES:

A FOCUS ON FACILITY MANAGEMENT

Second Edition

Paul David Platt

STRAIGHTFORWARD LEADERSHIP AND MANAGEMENT STRATEGIES:

A FOCUS ON FACILITY MANAGEMENT

Paul David Platt

© 2021 By Paul David Platt

All Rights Reserved

This book is dedicated to the hardworking people in the facility management industry. Often taken for granted, this dedicated group of people remain the behind-the-scenes lifeblood of virtually every facility around the globe.

Every effort has been made to make this publication to be as accurate as possible. The material within should not serve as the sole source of information of subject matter. The author shall have no liability or responsibility to any person or entity regarding any loss or damage incurred, or alleged to have incurred, either directly or indirectly, by any information contained herein.

CONTENTS

1. INTRODUCTION

2. LEADERSHIP VS. MANAGEMENT

3. FACILITY MANAGEMENT OVERVIEW

4. ORGANIZATIONAL LEADERSHIP & MORALE

5. CUSTOMERS & CLIENTS

6. TEAM MEMBERS

7. SELF-IMPROVEMENT

8. COMMUNICATION FUNDAMENTALS

9. REPUTATION & COMMITMENT

10. EMERGENCY MANAGEMENT & PLAN C

11. SAFETY-MINDED CULTURE

12. LESSONS LEARNED

13. SUMMARY OF TAKEAWAY MESSAGES

"You don't need a hundred reasons why something can't be done, just *one* reason why it should."

-author

1

Introduction

In this book, we do not go into each aspect of maintenance and custodial operations. There is a plethora of resources available for each of these niches. What we do focus on is the human factor, after all this is the true variable in the equation of any business entity. Products, machines, software, tools, etc. are considered more of the constants in this puzzle because even though technology or processes evolve, you essentially only need to keep up with the changes and continue onward. People are the most complex and remain the common denominator in all tasks and therefore are the most important assets we have in the world of facility management.

You, as the leader and manager, are vitally important to keeping a facility operating smoothly. The front-line employees are also just as critically important to an efficient organization. So, in this guide, we will focus on the management of yourself and the leadership of your team, because people are multifaceted and dynamic, and likely will remain the greatest consistent challenge you will encounter over the course of your career. To this end, we discuss the three main elements of people as applied to facility management in terms of the business realm: 1] the clients, 2] the employees, and 3] you, in the center of all this as the leader.

This condensed guide is purposely written in a straightforward and to-the-point style. Each chapter is narrowed down to only essential and relevant information that comes from a distillation of shared practices, ideas, knowledge, and insights gained over many years of real-world facility management and organizational leadership experience.

Included at the end of each chapter, there are key "takeaway messages" for further practical guidance. No unnecessary wordiness is intended or required. After all, we all have important work to do.

2

Leadership vs. Management

In the organizational leadership sphere, there is a supposed defining line between management and leadership. A manager is not the same as a leader and vice versa. The underlying logic for this is a leader influences the direction and vision of the organization and the manager conducts the daily operational tasks to keep the mission on track. This separation of how oversight is conducted holds true in many organizational structures.

Of course, in real life those lines of distinction are sometimes blurred because it is not realistic to expect a manager not to also lead and a leader to not also manage. This is especially true in the facility management world which demands a balance of managing *things* such as budgets, schedules, and all the systems that make up a building—its mechanical and electrical infrastructure that perpetuates its functional purpose—and also people—those individuals who are directly responsible for the caretaking of the facility as a whole. Those two entities of people and things intertwine quite often. The leadership role formulates the vision of the particulars that the facility management organization should be focused on—its path and direction. The manager role then takes over and makes all those things happen daily, in real time.

The textbook definitions of managers and leaders divide these roles as separate functions but in most facility management organizations these roles are doubled-up, blended to meet the dynamic requirements of the continually demanding facility management duties.

This is not intended to illustrate the differences of the two roles of control structure in an organization. On the contrary, the intent of what follows is to highlight ways of efficiency and effectiveness of these roles to be utilized as a merged leadership model—the manager as leader—in respect to the facility management industry.

Experience teaches us that the most effective person in an organization is the one who is capable both a leader and manager. The most ineffective one chooses to only be a leader or only a manager when the circumstances demand otherwise.

3

Facility Management Overview

At its core, facility management is essentially making a business entity work efficiently by taking care of every tangible item that affects its operations and activities. This can involve a multitude of assets in a facility—basically everything that you can see, and touch has an impact on the success of the business.

The facility management field covers a broad spectrum of skills, trades, and specialty knowledge. Over time, it requires you to become a subject matter expert in multiple areas. To be successful, you need to be adaptable, resourceful, and create a sound network of individuals and other resources that can assist in the specialized details. There is no conceivable way to become an expert in all fields related to facility management, but you will need to be, and can be concurrently knowledgeable and confident in multiple subject areas.

The following are limited, broad examples of the diverse areas involved within facility management. Each category has depth of its own and there are many areas that you will need to be well versed in at some point during your career. (Oftentimes, you will be personally involved in at least a dozen areas simultaneously).

- ✓ Code compliance
- ✓ Safety standards, awareness, and practices
- ✓ Custodial services
- ✓ Disaster recovery methods
- ✓ Electrical systems and troubleshooting
- ✓ Elevators and conveyance systems
- ✓ Emergency power generation
- ✓ Energy management
- ✓ Fire alarms and fire suppression systems
- ✓ Floor care and maintenance
- ✓ General construction methods

- ✓ Grounds and landscaping
- ✓ HVAC/R
- ✓ IT & infrastructure
- ✓ Lighting systems
- ✓ Locks, keys, security
- ✓ Moving, changes, and special events
- ✓ Plumbing systems
- ✓ Project planning and management
- ✓ Waste management & recycling services
- ✓ Preventative maintenance
- ✓ Capital renewal and reserve planning

Use all available resources to educate yourself on other areas that you may encounter. Don't be shy about shadowing contractors, technicians, consultants, or engineers while they are on your site. Ask questions whenever you have the opportunity. You may be surprised at how enthusiastic people are to talk about their field. Most take it as a compliment that you value their specialized knowledge, so use every available occasion to gather their insights, opinions, and recommendations. Knowing current trends and lessons learned from the general facility industry in addition to comparable facilities is a prime method of staying ahead of problems.

Become a proficient researcher and routinely read whatever relevant publication material you come across. Join online forums that specialize in your area of management. Invent a personal system to file information that may not be useful today but will probably come into play down the road. Electronic files, web page bookmarks, or traditional hard copies—whatever works best for you is the best way. Nothing beats having the information accessible and at the ready. A facility manager's comprehensive knowledge forms the foundation supporting the complexities that constitute a facility management organization's mission.

Takeaway messages:

1. Become knowledgeable and well versed.

2. If you do not know the answer, know how to find the answer.

3. Include outside service providers as sources of information.

4. Stay curious and informed.

4

Organizational Leadership & Morale

Understanding human relations within the context of an organization is a complex endeavor with all the intricacies of workplace dynamics, personalities, and differing management styles and philosophies. A most critical element within this multifaceted framework of an organization is leadership. Maintaining effective leadership is the capstone of any successful business entity. For this reason, it is crucial to understand your own personality, perceptions, values, and self-concepts to become an exemplary leader.

Fortunately, great leadership is a skill that can be learned. The first aspect of improving leadership is coming to terms with your own strengths and weaknesses, knowing what they are and how to leverage them are a crucial part of self-improvement. Authentic leaders are more genuine and aware of their strengths, limitations, and emotions. For instance, by experiencing my share of poor methods of motivational attempts over the years and experiencing leaders who strictly rely on disciplinary tactics or intimidation methods, I have used these negative examples of "what not to do" to craft my own motivation philosophies. You can always learn from others.

The second part of cultivating great leadership is relying on the foundational principles of leadership. These areas include four main pillars—leading by example, inspiring the team, challenging the norm, and leading with empathy. Knowing these skills and applying them within your organization will generate positive outcomes.

Leading by example is crucial because people react to actual behavior from their leaders versus superficial personalities or promises. Model the behavior you expect. Maintaining a high standard of ethics and values remain the core principles of good character. The concept of moral integrity deeply impacts decision-making practices because each decision has an effect on reputation and trust. Earning the respect of others is paramount in keeping the willful trust of constituents. Values such as honesty, transparency, and trustworthiness are a part of this framework. Building and maintaining mutual trust is imperative for organizational success.

Inspiring the team involves conveying a shared vision of the goals which creates a sense of commonality with the group. It is important to clearly convey your vision of purpose and mission. Who are we, what do we value, what do we want to accomplish, and where are we headed? These are the vital questions to provide the answers to when formulating your vision of the organization. Try authentic storytelling as a technique to inspire and personalize your organizational vision. People can more easily relate to personable stories such as anecdotes, or even parables to "picture" the message. All will be more receptive to advancing a mission that contains a shared goal. It gives the sense that "we're in this together". Great leaders can make their leadership passionate and personal so others care about the vision and the mission of the whole.

By providing others a reason to care about the goals set forth, unity will be promoted without forcing it. Those team members will be the ones who implement the vision you have communicated and by them envisioning the end result, everyone can work towards achieving a positive outcome. If genuine passion can be effectively expressed for your organizational vision, the purposefulness and combined energy from the team will naturally follow.

Challenging the norm involves taking calculated risks and learning from those experiences when things do not work out as expected. Never concede with remaining stagnant and only relying on your own skills and experience. Achievement may not be possible without enduring challenges and seeking assistance and knowledge from others when necessary. Do the same for subordinates and assign them projects, not just a list of tasks. The bottom line is challenges and risks should be viewed as opportunities to improve, not as things to be feared. Successfully working through challenges ultimately empowers you and your team.

Displaying empathy is sometimes overlooked in the daily business world and it should be the opposite—it should be an integral part of doing business. You lead with empathy when you bring out the best in others and give them the confidence to succeed. Offer encouragement when needed and openly give recognition to others when deserved. Providing opportunities for others to make decisions enables them to act and helps to build confidence. Your demonstration of confidence in their abilities enables them to perform at their best levels. Acknowledging the viewpoints of others and validating them as being important will strengthen the cohesiveness of the team and therefore, the shared vision of the mission.

Instead of supplying answers to subordinates, take a step back and allow yourself time to ask questions about their way of thinking and their ideas about solving a problem. This trust will give them the confidence needed to enable action. This is especially important in the facilities management world because creative thinking is often required for solving complex technical problems that usually occur under urgent time constraints. Having the team accustomed to thinking on their feet is an obvious advantage when critical situations arise.

Be an empathetic leader by showing genuine concern for the problems and aspirations subordinates have by having personal face-to-face conversations. This opens the communication channel so information can flow more freely because of trust and familiarity. If opportunities are utilized correctly and with genuineness, you will enable a higher level of performance. If sincere concern is shown toward others, then trustworthiness is signaled within the group, and trust is built organically inside the organization. Spending time to get to know your team and what their challenges and interests are goes against the traditional authoritarian leadership style, which seldom does not deliver favorable long-term outcomes. It only makes sense that you must be close to a situation to fully understand it. The same holds true for relationships with people. The bottom line is, if you take the time to listen to others, they will take the time to listen to you.

One of the most important functions of a good manager is being a good leader. Being a good manager does not automatically make you a good leader. Lead by example. Lead with vision. Lead with empathy.

Both the leader and manager have an overwhelming impact on morale, and thus, productivity. Happy and content employees simply perform better and are more reliable. The less stress employees have, the less stress you will have.

Great Leaders:

- Inspire excellence—a high bar of achievement eventually becomes the reality

- Inspire growth of their employees—build needed skills while mitigating negative behavior

- Ensure accountability—the team and the individual deliver on their promises

- Encourage teamwork—trust and respect go a lot further than competitive behavior does

- Build positive relationships—those same time-honored relationships will protect you when you fumble

You constantly need to be in the mindset of problem solver. Always focus on the root of problems by asking "why" instead of "who". Your goal should be to find the cause of issues versus looking for targets to blame. This is the only way to find an effective and permanent solution.

Plan to be replaced. If you are not thinking this way, you are in for an awakening later. You should select and mentor your successor. This accomplishes several things of benefit:

- First, it does not limit your career progression as employers need to know there is a competent and workable succession plan—you cannot be promoted if there is no one identified to seamlessly take over your current responsibilities.

- Secondly, it gives you an extra layer of support from the junior manager—

they will do whatever to help you succeed because they know they are essentially helping themselves progress in their own career.

- Thirdly, it relieves some workload from your plate as the aspiring manager should eagerly take on more and more tasks and responsibilities.

Be Humble

Another important trait in a good leader is knowing that you do not have to win every disagreement or respond to every criticism. Be self-effacing and humble. A great leader is confident and secure enough to admit fault and ask for help when necessary. Do not let ego get in the way of competent leadership.

Judgment

Exercising sound judgment comes from experience, wisdom, and knowledge gained over the years. Making impactful decisions is part of the daily routines as a facility manager. This is a huge responsibility that should not be taken lightly. Rely on your strengths and seek guidance whenever unsure. Never be too proud to ask for a second opinion.

Team Morale

An example of poor leadership cultivating an organization with low satisfaction and morale rates is one where over-management or micro-management tendencies are abused. The employee is constantly pressured and feels the level of trust is undermined. Giving autonomy to employees is one of the best ways to enhance job satisfaction and increase motivation and performance. Ensure everyone knows *what* they are doing and *why* they are doing it provides intention and direction.

These philosophies translate well within the team and builds a high level of trust and morale. Team members know, by firsthand knowledge that their interests are being considered, not just the one-sided ask from the organization.

Eliminating as much unnecessary stress is an important factor for increasing motivation and productivity. And since a lot of our time is spent in the workplace, organizations understandably have a huge impact on employees' overall stress and wellbeing. For this reason alone, workplace stress should be mitigated as much as possible to promote healthy, happy, loyal, and productive employees.

Setting the example and realizing that a positive attitude coupled with motivations and energy from the leader will reciprocate and create a cycle of high morale and performance. Ensure any obstacles are removed that may hinder employees from achieving the desired results. This sets everyone up for success, which promotes further trust and harmony of the team.

A good rule is to always make a conscious effort to place yourself into your individual team member's perspectives:

1. *How are you perceived?*

2. *Are your directives clear?*
3. *Is there a well-communicated vision?*
4. *Do your overall priorities align with individual tasks?*

In more cases than not, employees with high morale will consistently go above and beyond to exceed your expectations.

- A high morale environment establishes confident employees—everyone is secure in their standing.

- It fosters enthusiastic employees—people enjoy coming to work versus dreading the workplace (and miss less days as a result)

- It provides the framework for disciplined employees.

The old business analogy of "people will buy from someone they like" applies in the same way. If your employees like you, they will produce results for you. Do not underestimate this fact, and certainly, whatever you do, do not abuse it or take people for granted. Your respected status will quickly dissolve.

Takeaway messages:

1. *Lead by example and empathy.*

2. *Lead with a clear, communicated vision.*

3. *Offer encouragement when needed and openly give recognition to others when deserved.*

4. *Have a succession plan.*

5. *Eliminate causes of unnecessary workplace stress.*

6. *Do not let ego impede true leadership*

5

Customers & Clients

An important realization to acknowledge is that you not only have to lead and manage employees, but you also must manage your customers and clients. Management of your customers is a vital, but an often-overlooked aspect. The number one rule is to listen and respond appropriately. Remember, competence, consistency, and quality will win over clients at the end of the day. You must build trust.

By contemplating the following three questions, you will always be set on the right track:

1. ***What is their issue or complaint?***
   Understanding the core complaint is key to determining an agreeable solution. This is where listening and asking follow-up questions is necessary to gather all pertinent information comes into play.

2. ***How are you going to resolve their issue?*** Once you have a sound understanding of the problem, a plan of action can be formulated for the best resolution.

3. ***How are you going to communicate the resolution?*** If the solution is complex or will take multiple steps, that action plan should be communicated as early and as often as possible to the customer or client.

You must remember the customer has a wholly different perspective and motives than you do. Place yourself in their position and try to understand the situation from their viewpoint. A sound, permanent resolution to the problem is the goal. Never offer up "false assurances" (a term that will be used again in another section) just to appease the customer in the short term. You do not want to revisit the same issue a week or even a year from now and most importantly, you do not want to lose their trust.

Generally, there are two basic types of customers and we will discuss their traits and the best methods to manage their general tendencies and actions. There is the one type of customer who complains and the one who does not—commonly referred to as "the walker" and "the talker". Keep in mind a person can fluctuate between the two types of customers and therefore an individual should not be grouped permanently into one category or the other. Your reaction will be based upon their communicative style for the given situation.

The Walker

The most dangerous type of customer is arguably the walker. This is the one that may bring an issue to your attention subtly or may never actually verbalize or communicate that anything is wrong. They will basically give you one shot to get it right. You may never even know the issue or the complaint. They can and will, unexpectedly up and leave as a customer, or more commonly in the facilities world, seek to replace you as their service provider.

The Talker

The "talker" customer complains openly and freely. This is a good thing, and you should treat the situation as such. They are giving you an opportunity to correct something that, in their perception, is not right. You are never forced to guess about the problem. If it is a repeat complaint, you need to re-evaluate your past "solution" and find the permanent fix. Spending the time and energy on this now will save you bucket loads of stress later.

So, what can you do about the walker?

Simply concentrate your efforts on what you can control. Deliver what was promised and maintain proactive communication when things do go wrong. Things will go wrong. This is where establishing a solid reputation will pay dividends. Again, focus on what you can control and deliver to the best of your ability. Reasonably, this is all that can be asked of anyone.

What about the talker?

Although overbearing at times, the talker is your best customer in terms of opportunity for success when problems occur. Look at it this way—they are giving you every opportunity to correct something, essentially giving you second and third chances to get it right. Ensure that you effectively listen to their complaint and execute an agreeable solution. Communicate with them through the whole process as they thrive on interaction and feedback.

In the end, it is all about forming a positive partnership experience with your client or customer. Seek opportunities to enhance services or expand support whenever and wherever possible. Consistent trust building and offering an excellent communication chain are the core factors of the partnership. A symbiotic business relationship with the client is the ultimate goal.

Takeaway messages:

1. Listen and understand the problem, then find an acceptable resolution.

2. Learn early on what type of customers or clients you have and tailor your leadership and management style to fit accordingly.

3. Proactive communication is essential when problems are encountered.

4. Remember, competence, consistency, and quality wins over clients at the end of the day.

6

Team Members

Building and maintaining an effective team is paramount. You cannot control every decision and judgment, so it is crucial to build and maintain a trustworthy team. So how do you do that? First and foremost, whenever you have an opportunity to add or replace employees, there are two important attributes in selecting a solid candidate in addition to the normal training and experience requisites.

This is referred to as the "Two I's". These are innate traits that cannot be taught or learned on the job. Essentially, a person either willfully has these qualities or they do not, so once you identify personnel that possesses the "Two I's", do what it takes to keep them and grow them on your team.

The "Two I's"

- The best employee is one that has <u>initiative</u>. While other skills can be taught, initiative is something that someone either has or they do not. You can do without an employee that gives you excuses why something was not or could not be accomplished. You need the type of team player that can understand the reason why it should be done. They do what is needed without being asked. The value of this cannot be overstated.

- <u>Integrity</u> is also key. If you constantly must check behind someone or worry if a task is getting accomplished correctly, then you have the wrong employee. Second guessing yourself is one thing, but not having confidence in what you are being told or promised leads to trouble. We call this the 80% employee—one who consistently overestimates their performance by 20% or only delivers 80% of their potential. You want someone who delivers 100%, even when there is no one checking. Trust in your team is crucial to building trust with your client.

Team Building

Facility management requires a diversely skilled group of individuals to work in synchronous fashion to accomplish a mission. Solid leadership that involves team building and an open feedback loop helps to form a smoothly functioning and productive facility management organization. A cohesive, mission-focused group is imperative for continued success. This requires teamwork. Building the necessary team structure requires using several leadership practices, all beginning with the character and values of the leader.

Feedback to team members is critical for growth and development within the facility management organization. Accurate, timely, back-and-forth information is imperative for the dynamic demands of the job. Keep people focused on what they can control and do not let their goals get sidelined by distractions.

An important aspect of the feedback loop is making it safe for people to experiment and take risks by promoting learning from their experiences. So much more can be accomplished by working together and this can only be done with an open communication.

Team Talent

Talent acquisition is a key part of running a successful team. A good tip to finding skilled and employable individuals is to simply look around your larger facility management world. A great source is someone that is working for a similar company or a skilled tradesperson that is currently working for a contractor. These people are highly employable because they are already working, and therefore obviously have the skills and certifications that are inherent and required to be successful within their field.

Remember, it will be a tremendous waste of your time and energy if you think you can change personality or character traits. Initiative needs to be built-in to what team members are expected to do. Instead, focus on what you can change: people's technical skill levels, decision making processes, time management techniques, etc. These are aspects that are teachable and trainable. This all can be accomplished through learned behavior—training, repetition, and practical experience.

What is an obvious sign of an effective team? An effective team can operate without you on the short term. This is important for not only your peace of mind, but also the client's. Stakeholders need to feel assured that things will continue to operate smoothly under varying circumstances. And when you have placed the right people in the right positions and have empowered them with the appropriate training, experience opportunities, and proper guidance, your team will function in a near self-sufficient capacity.

This does not threaten your job security, it only enhances it. Exemplary leaders constantly put the work in on the front end and the results will speak for themselves. Effective team building is accomplished as a continual long-term process and when executed effectively, is a highly sought-after skill in leaders.

Retaining Employees

Employee retention and workforce turnover is directly impacted by your leadership and management style and the workplace atmosphere you help to create. You are the responsible party for creating a positive working environment.

Talk to your employees, show genuine interest in some aspect of their life beyond work. This does not have to be intrusive—something as simple as knowing general facts about their family or a hobby they enjoy. This helps to create a caring atmosphere that will translate into better performance because if the employee gets the sense that you do not care about them personally, what is their motivation to go above and beyond to help you shine?

Surveys and research have shown that the number one reason employees are unhappy in a job is oftentimes not monetarily based. Frequently it is based on job satisfaction and feeling included as part of a team. Everyone wants to feel their efforts are part of something bigger, even if it means the role they currently perform is not the role they desire to be in a year or two from now. Most individuals want a career, not just a job. They must know they have opportunities for advancement and progression within their skill, trade, or industry.

Allowing input in workplace actions and decisions, even simple ones, goes a long way towards making an employee feel included, valued, and secure in their career.

Balance Feedback

Corrective actions are unavoidable and necessary, but be just as generous with praise, recognition, and reward when things go well. Human nature is much more receptive to positive feedback versus the converse. Building up an employee's morale by simply saying "great job" when everything goes as planned is a painless, but effective means to reinforce appreciation. Be sincere and genuine about the delivery of congratulatory remarks. An employee who feels appreciated in the workplace will always do more than is expected.

Use shortfalls in performance as opportunities for training or re-training. You will find that most people respond positively when expectations of them are made abundantly clear. This empowers them with the confidence in knowing the parameters for their own success.

High Turnover

An important point: if you are experiencing a high rate of employee turnover, then odds are you could be directly or indirectly a part of the reason. You solve a high turnover problem with finding the root cause of the trend. If you immediately blame each employee's departure on placing fault, you will never resolve the inherent reason of why they chose to leave.

Make yourself accessible. Employees need to know you have an open-door policy. Sometimes being available to listen to grievances or complaints will make all the difference in creating a more positive attitude in the workplace. The word will spread organically that leadership views everyone as individual people and not just bodies to complete tasks. Sometimes we forget that everyone has a life outside of the workplace and you never know what someone may be going through on a personal level. Take the time and make the effort to understand the people on your team.

Do not make the mistake of misjudging an employee's poor performance solely on them. It may be due to failure on your part to clearly communicate the mission or assigned duty. Remember that everyone does not think exactly like you do and there are multiple ways to correctly complete a task. Your way is not always the only way. Ensure your team has the appropriate training, equipment, and clear direction that is necessary to complete what is being expected of them.

Be open and receptive to any innovative ideas someone may bring to the table. Make sure to give due credit to the individual in a public company setting (such as a team meeting) to display the proper acknowledgement and appreciation for their efforts.

Cultivating Level 5 Employees

The path from a beginner to a seasoned expert is long, but not at all linear. It's a relatively fast path when someone is starting from zero knowledge and experience to the next level of progression. Any training or knowledge gained is 100% more than they had previously.

The progression from level three to level five is exponentially more difficult. The average, or (above average) well-performing employee usually plateaus at level three or four. The journey from level four to even the bottom tier of level five is the toughest road.

It requires an absolute commitment and a high level of self-motivation to continue upward, from both the employee and the employer. It will not happen without effort and sacrifices beyond the normal workday.

Here is a brief overview of typical employee progression tier categories:

Level 1—This is the beginner or novice, with some training, but no experience; or has some experience, but no fundamental training

Level 2—Fastest growth tier, information is being absorbed rapidly and skills are becoming honed

Level 3—Solid, dependable fundamental skills, but not ready to take on the responsibility of decision making yet

Level 4—Capable of leading others, solves more complex problems, begins to think long-game, plans and lays out work projects, uses sound judgment in decisions

Level 5—Subject matter expert, capable of independent command of their field, responds well to high-stress situations, proficient in making advanced level decisions and judgment calls; finds and implements solutions to simultaneous problems

3 C's Needed for Successful Progression

The high potential, engaged employee will need to maintain a few fundamental traits throughout their progression journey:

1. Commit:
    1. to your responsibilities.
    2. to better yourself.
    3. to delivering quality work.
2. Communicate:
    1. what others need to know.
    2. what you need to know from others.
3. Care:
    1. about doing a good job.
    2. about your work ethic.
    3. about the success of all.

Remember, the formula for achievement and success involves other inherent attributes other than talent, knowledge, education, or experience. The following five things require none of that, but are equally important in the success formula:

1. **Showing up** (be on time and be present, in mind and body)
2. **Working hard** (work ethic, deliver 100% of your capability)
3. **Attitude** (initiative, positive thinking)
4. **Passion** (care about the impact your work has on others)

Preparation (be ready and stay ready)

These ideas are useful to share with employees to motivate and empower them. There is no substitute for hard work and no mystery formula to being successful. A great reminder for all of us.

Takeaway messages:

1. An exceptional employee cares about doing a good job. Everything matters to them and they pay attention to the details.

2. Once you find a high performing employee, do what it takes to keep them and grow them on your team.

3. Do not make the mistake of misjudging an employee's poor performance due to failure on your part to clearly communicate the mission.

4. A smoothly functioning organization involves team building and an open feedback loop.

5. Avoid excessive turnover by creating a positive atmosphere that rewards success.

6. An inclusive, team-oriented workplace is vital for content employees.

7. Empower employees by demonstrating they have a career progression path.

7

Self-Improvement

Oftentimes, the first place to look to solve many issues is within. Maybe you are part of the problem. And if you are part of the problem, that also means that you can be part of the solution.

A constant seeking of self-improvement in skills, knowledge, and abilities, will help pull others surrounding you to do the same. Learn, adapt, and grow all that you can. Encourage building off the small wins to cultivate even greater successes. Remember that long-term strategies are oftentimes the best short-term strategies in building a successful organization and this applies to yourself as well.

Does the employee have the training and proper tools to complete the job? Are your directives clear? Sometimes your vision of something does not translate well to the front-line employee. You cannot fairly and justly hold someone accountable for something if they did not receive adequate training or have not been supplied with the right tools and equipment to get the job done. Identifying shortfalls and providing the essentials is part of your responsibilities as a leader. Think in terms of a servant-leader where your primary role is to ensure subordinates have the best chance of success in their mission by being attended to by you.

Getting your expectations and vision across to the ones completing the work is paramount. Take an honest look at your communication style. Are you being clear with the instructions? Be accurate and concise—do not confuse people with extra details or inadequate instructions.

It is your function to properly coordinate work efforts so everything is completed safely and effectively. If you must break complex jobs up into smaller, more manageable tasks, so be it. That is also your job as a leader. Putting in the time and planning upfront will pay dividends in time and stress saved later.

A personal motto I use is "*You don't need a hundred reasons why something can't be done, just <u>one</u> reason why you should*". This fits for you as well as your employees, but it always starts with you. Never give up before any attempt is made. You should take failures as lessons and find a better way. Don't be afraid to seek assistance if needed. You will not automatically know the solution to everything that you encounter. You are a facility professional because you know how to find and implement solutions. Use the resources around you, from your own employees to the wealth of knowledge available online. If you come across something that you don not quite understand, it should bother you enough to conduct research to find the answers. You should always be thirsty for knowledge.

Never get comfortable or complacent with your position. You should always have this fact in mind: everyone is replaceable. This should not give you anxiety, but on the contrary, it should keep you motivated and driven. Stretch and challenge yourself and always look to improve your knowledge and skills. Create reasonable goals for yourself and never accept that you have learned enough or gained enough experience. Invest in your intellectual capital.

Self-identify your strengths and weaknesses so that you can enhance what you excel at and improve in the areas that you do not. Stay inquisitive and read everything you can about a variety of topics within your industry. You will be surprised at how something you read months ago may become relevant and useful to you in the future.

Time and task management is a must. There are countless publications written on the subject, but the simple message here is <u>do not procrastinate</u>. In the fast-paced world of facility management, a task put off until tomorrow translates into a quick march toward chaos and failure. No matter how small or trivial seeming they may seem, do not put off tasks. Tomorrow always brings more unexpected issues that will accumulate quickly on top of everything you failed to finish today.

Emergencies are not planned, so the expression, "make hay while the sun is shining" applies soundly. Do the mundane tasks while you have downtime because that next emergency is right around the corner. If you deal with items relatively immediately as they come to your attention, everything and everyone will run smoother. This strategy uses a prioritized approach to allow you to focus on the "now". It also avoids unnecessary "piling up" of work on employees at the last minute to make up for your looming deadline. This never goes over well in any respect.

An effective strategy is to use the early morning hours or after shift hours to formulate needed planning for the day ahead, or for the following workday.

This method works because it places you in the work mindset and allows time for you to concentrate without the distractions that happen during "normal" business hours.

Plan far enough ahead to keep on schedule, but always leave room for the unexpected requests or emergencies. If you are in control of your schedule, why set yourself up for failure by overbooking your time?

Seamless Function

Take the following statement under consideration and evaluate your program: Don't mistake being needed all the time under the same pretense of being a valuable leader or manager. It should give you pause If you are told that things "fall apart" when you are not around. Though this can ostensibly seem as flattering, but this should be taken as a red flag warning that things are not operating as smoothly as they could be.

As mentioned in the *Employee* chapter, if you have managed, planned, and directed everything correctly, then operations should not rapidly fall in disarray when you are not around. The goal is to have everyone properly trained and informed so there is a seamless function when you are away.

Surround Yourself with Challengers

This one should be taken as hard advice. It sometime becomes beneficial to surround yourself with people who do not always agree with your ideas. Listening to the ideas and viewpoints of those who do not agree with you because they care more about the overall success of the organizational mission can be invaluable.

When you only surround yourself with "yes" people, you may become disillusioned into a false sense of success. When you allow yourself to become comfortable, you become complacent. When you become complacent, failure is imminent.

Takeaway messages:

1. *Constantly stretch yourself and stay curious to constantly grow and evolve. Learn, adapt, and develop all that you can.*

2. *Encourage building off the small wins to cultivate even greater successes.*

3. *Remember that long-term strategies are oftentimes the best short-term strategies*

4. *Focus on the root of problems versus directing blame.*

5. *Do not procrastinate.*

6. *Don't force your "failure to plan" work on your employees.*

7. *Ensure seamless function. If you have managed, planned, and directed everything right, then operations should not fall apart when you're not present.*

8. *It can be beneficial to surround yourself with people who do not always agree with your ideas so differing perspectives can be offered.*

8

Communication Fundamentals

Just as in any business, communication is key to long term success in facility management. In the facility world, it is even more imperative for communication to flow quickly and efficiently between you and the client, and between you and the front-line employee. Here are the major points to remember and put into practice:

- Learn what to communicate and when to communicate it.
- Learn your employees and learn your client.
- Too much information is sometimes just as bad as not enough.
- As a rule, communicate what you would want to know if you were in the other person's role.

- Employees deserve to know the big picture of why they do certain things. It will help morale and performance because they will have a feeling of inclusion and a sense of purpose versus just completing repetitive or mundane tasks. (This impacts not only employee performance, but also employee retention).

- Clearly communicate your vision to the departmental level. Tailor it to only essential information so it is appropriate and applicable to only what is needed.

Effective Use of E-mail

E-mail is by far the most prevalent form of communication in the business world. Since it is such a common form of correspondence, we will go more in depth. Here are a few tips that will keep you an effective email communicator:

1. Compose brief, concise messages. Do not over-explain things and do not attempt to use unnecessary or "big" words when a more common word will do just fine. More than likely, you will come across as trying

to "sound smart" which makes you look just the opposite. If it takes more than four or five paragraphs, then a meeting or phone call may be warranted.

2. Use your judgment on what your customer is more comfortable with. An easy way to get a feel for what the customer wants is to simply read the emails they send. Are they concise, or are they lengthy? Do they open with a drawn-out explanation, or is the first line the point? You will do well to take notice of different styles and adapt as well.

3. Remember, e-mail is not in the same professional hierarchy as phone texts or other forms of instant messaging. Do not fall into the trap of texting when an e-mail is more appropriate. Know when to use both and do not compose an e-mail with the same abbreviations and phrasing as a text.

4. <u>Always</u> use proper grammar and spelling. (Even if the customer doesn't. They don't have to.)

5. Another mistake made with e-mail is the response time. An e-mail does not have to be responded to immediately—that is the purpose of phone calls and texts. Take the time to read and comprehend what someone is communicating and then respond accordingly. Simply firing off a quick reply in the interest of being super responsive will lead to trouble. You may convey incorrect or incomplete information.

6. Simply responding "Okay", "Will do", or "Got it" usually results in inaction to occur because the responder completely forgot about the message. Once they sent a response, it has a high probability of going completely off their radar.

7. One of the worst responses you could send in most situations is the

one-word response of "Noted". This could be perceived by the reader as non-committal and vague at best, flippant and contrived at worst. There are certainly instances where this response could be appropriate, just use caution.

8. Be careful with the use of "reply all". Replying to all in a group is intended to streamline a group conversation with a single communication thread. You may not always know all parties included or their role. This is where it becomes even more crucial to use short, accurate, and grammatically correct responses. If something needs to be communicated to a select group, a new email chain is recommended. This precludes any potential conflict or unintended consequences of a misunderstanding of others on the original group communication.

9. Here is a great tip for knowing when to respond in a group conversation:

if you are not directly addressed in the conversation or are only included in the "C.c." address, stay out of the conversation unless you are directly addressed in the body of the email. The message's probable intent is to inform you rather than illicit a response or ask for your input.

10. Shy away from blind copying other parties on your e-mail. This will inevitably lead to trouble sooner or later. Use sparingly and decisively.

Verbal Conversations

Always be vigilant and conscious of your professional bearing. Keep both phone and in-person conversations on the business level. Do not make the mistake of perceiving a false degree of comfort with clients or employees. You run the risk of misreading the other person's level of acceptable informality. The safe bet is to keep it about business and remain consistently cordial and professional.

Communication Standards

Communication is the fundamental element of business. Effective communication, no matter the method of transmission, is important to meet several criteria to have the expected outcome. Communication should be:

- Clear – your message needs to be easily understood.
- Concise – brevity and simplicity are the goals
- Objective – do not add your opinion when unwarranted
- Consistent – reliable, steady messaging prevents confusion
- Complete – a well-defined message should be comprehensive to include any expected responses or actions. Start with the end result in mind. What is your objective?
- Relevant – the message timing and content should make sense to the receiver
- Consider the knowledge of the audience – do not over or under

explain. Tailor your message to your target audience.

Communication Channels

To ensure effective communication, the sender needs to consider the method of communication and select the appropriate means for the context.

Text messaging

It is less disruptive than a phone call and more immediate than an email message. Use sparingly or as the situation dictates.

Email

It is the ubiquitous choice for business for speed and accessibility for the sender and receiver.

Face-to-Face

Allow the use of all the senses and provides instant and continuous feedback

Group communication

Allows for the highest degree of collaboration and idea sharing while offering timely feedback to the group. The group combines their strengths and perspectives to efficiently arrive at a desired outcome.

Informal Communication

People are connected through communication and each one of us is a sender and a receiver of constant messaging that takes many forms. It is a mistake to communicate only through the formal organizational channels. Informal social networks are just as important to the success of an organization because the majority of the constituents communicate in a more verbal, informal manner. Leverage the opportunities this can provide for you to reach the entire team. This is where your leadership values can provide results by reaching those who may not have the same access as other members of the organization. Informal peer groups encourage collaboration and teamwork. Informal communication should complement the formal channels of communication and be utilized as another method for success. These informal peer groups will exist with or without you, so it is best to capitalize on the value they can bring with magnifying and reinforcing your message or organizational culture.

The Communication Process

A good first step in communication is confirming that the entire organization is on the same page with the end results in mind. Everyone on the team should fully understand what the objectives are to ensure efforts are being focused towards a common goal.

The communication process serves three main goals in any organization. It allows for coordination of efforts, it relays information, and it afford the sharing of emotions and feelings among employees. A lack of any of these elements will lead to disruption and inefficiency. Simply put, people must know what, when, where, and how to complete a given task. With this, it becomes clear that communication is the heart of organizations.

Real world examples in facility management include barriers formed from filtered information. To fulfill a request from a customer, clear facts are imperative in finding a solution and providing an agreeable outcome. Many times, clients tend not to explain their issues very well and it takes extra effort to figure out exactly what is wanted. Often, in cases where only verbal messages are transmitted, the physical location of the work or the scope of the problem is not well communicated. This leads to lost time and productivity, and in some cases, work performed in the wrong area or on the wrong equipment. The client is not happy for obvious reasons and neither is the employee, who may feel they have wasted their time.

By being a good leader, you can use a more effective communication process to positively impact the outcomes by minimizing filtered or misinformation. From a pure efficiency standpoint, this not only makes logical sense, but also benefits the frontline employees performing the work by boosting their overall morale and job satisfaction knowing they can trust the information received. Without effective communication, the basics of the work at hand could never be completed, leading to unhappy customers and disengaged employees. Therefore, the transfer of communication to the client is just as important as the transfer of information to the frontline employees.

Takeaway messages:

1. *Use grammatically correct, concise, and accurate replies.*

2. *Take the time to fully comprehend what the client is communicating and then respond thoughtfully and appropriately.*

3. *Respond only when addressed directly or when otherwise necessary to add value to the conversation.*

4. *Use caution with use of "reply all" and B.c.c.*

5. *Use professionalism with all communication channels.*

6. *Leverage informal communication opportunities that can provide benefit for the entire team.*

7. *A good first step in communication is confirming that the entire organization is on the same page with the end results in mind.*

9

Reputation & Commitment

Your reputation is paramount. You need to reach the point of people consistently trusting your words because they have experienced a history of trusting your actions. You can easily develop your reputation by simply following through with what you promised. If you tell someone you are going to do something, do it. This may sound over simplified, but it only takes one instance of not delivering and your reputation is immediately tarnished, especially early on in a business relationship. You earn "passes" for legitimate mistakes only after years of demonstrated commitment and follow through.

Read this exaggerated example:

A man finally gets the courage to go sky diving and inquires at a local jump school about what is involved. The manager explained the procedures and precautions taken, "We expertly pack the parachutes and have never had a failure. We take you up and tell you when to jump. You pull the main ripcord; it always works, but if it doesn't, you pull the secondary chute ripcord. You float softly to the ground and we will meet you in that truck over there."

The man decides to give it a try. He boards the plane and it circles the airfield. He jumps out and the main chute fails. He pulls the auxiliary ripcord and that fails.

He looks down at the ground and says, "I bet that damned truck isn't there either."

-Unknown

Sure, a story intended for humor, but there are lessons to be learned from this tale. Lessons such as:

1. Establishing protocols and following through with them.
2. Having a method of checks and balances and accountability measures in place.
3. Avoiding complacency of relying on past successes.

In the world of facility management, always keep this fact in the forefront of your mind: you are responsible for the safety and well-being of many other individuals.

Following through and following up are imperative in facilities management. Some tasks have a higher priority or of greater importance, and for these types, always take the extra steps. Follow through with your employees and then make sure to follow up with the client to ensure nothing was overlooked.

Don't fall into the common trap of simply offering false assurances. The adage of "don't over-promise and under-deliver" still holds true.

Here is a less dramatic real-world scenario:

The client sends an email that requests the lighting to be checked in conference room 2B. There are multiple overhead lights out. Being the overzealous manager, you reply immediately with "I'll take care of it."

You want to project instantaneous service by offering a speedy response. The problem is, immediately after you send the email, you receive an emergency call about leaking water in the women's restroom on the third floor. Being the responsive manager, you instantly go into rescue mode to handle the water emergency. Now that the email has been read and responded to, you move on to the new emergency. The lights are overlooked, and the client must call you a second time to remind you before her meeting begins. Your reputation just suffered a blow.

Demonstrate commitment to your employees and customers. Show that you care about your employees' achievements and well-being. Demonstrate that you care about your client's business and success. The same commitment you show others will translate back favorably to you. After all, remember that your longevity and success is directly correlated with both your team's success and your client's success.

It's a tough world in facility management and it is also human nature for people to remember your failures or undelivered promises more than your achievements and wins. This is a fact of life and provides more reason to establish a sound reputation for following through and keeping your commitments. This is the best way to alleviate potential fallout from inevitable future stumbles.

Remember, just as competence, consistency, and quality wins over and keeps customers, it also wins over employees and everyone else around you.

Takeaway messages:

1. *Keep your promises to your clients and your employees.*

2. *Be committed.*

3. *Follow-through and follow-up.*

10

Emergency Management & Plan C

Emergency situations will arise and usually at the most inopportune times. What do you do when critical HVAC equipment fails? How do you handle water damage and cleanup? These are questions you will most likely have answers to but take it a step further and throw the same scenario within the worst timing context.

What do you do when everyone has already clocked out, or if something breaks down over the long holiday weekend? What do you do if a plumbing pipe bursts in the middle of the night?

Plan C is emergency management that has a backup plan. Plan A is normal operations, Plan B is the reaction to disruption of that normalcy, Plan C is what happens when resources aren't available to execute Plan B. The successful facility manager has plan C ideas already formulated.

Work out solutions to what keeps you up at night. Then delve deeper and think about what *should* be keeping you up at night. The time to figure out the "what if's" is right now. It is worlds easier to think of solutions when everything is going right versus during chaos and calamity.

Also, think about what to do in a 'triage' situation—when you have multiple emergency situations at once. Plan what would be the order of your priorities. Protecting building occupant's life and safety is always number one on the list. But what do you do if you have a power outage and catastrophic flooding happening at once? This is a very likely scenario in times of inclement weather. The point here is to be prepared for the chain of events that can quickly follow the initial catastrophe.

Here is a real-world example:

Due to severe weather events, your region experiences widespread power blackouts and you have critical equipment in your building's basement. The power outages could last several days. You need to keep critical equipment running or at least protected from water damage. The building's emergency generator will run out of fuel after 24 hrs. and resupply is not guaranteed. What's Plan C?

Plan B was good only for the first day. What is the plan to keep valuable equipment protected and the basement from flooding after 72 hours? This would be a Plan C scenario.

Make sure to schedule periodic "dry-runs" of actions in response to conceivable emergencies. This will identify shortcomings in the plan and inventory. Make sure to practice sound preventative maintenance on emergency equipment to make sure everything stays reliable.

A few tips:

- Organize a special response team—people you can depend on in high stress, fast paced situations.

- Keep essential back up parts and supplies on hand. Your normal methods of procurement may not be available.

- Determine if having specialized disaster recovery equipment is right for your facility. (Machines for water pick-up, dehumidifiers, gas-powered pumps, generators, blowers, etc.)

- Practice the plan using a dry-run approach. Usually it is the simple things that become the potential "showstoppers". These exercises will identify such issues.

- Keep the backup equipment and supplies maintained and checked periodically.

Hopefully, plan C scenarios will never have to be implemented, but preparedness is crucial. Even if you never execute the plan under emergency conditions, the side benefit to these planning and dry-run exercises usually results in identifying other vulnerabilities in your normal, day-to-day facility management plan.

Takeaway messages:

1. *Identify potential problem areas—both the obvious and not so obvious.*

2. *Practice the response periodically as a dry-run emergency exercise.*

3. *Maintain an adequate emergency equipment inventory.*

4. *Perform routine preventative maintenance to ensure reliability.*

11

Safety-Minded Culture

Everything else loses its perceived importance once someone gets injured. In the introduction, facilities management was mentioned as having people as the most important asset. This cannot be truer when it comes down to everyone's health and safety.

You will hear it emphasized over and again, but for good reason. Ensure you are familiar with OSHA standards. These are the minimum guidelines, so going above and beyond these guidelines is a good thing.

This is an area that ties in with all other aspects of the facility management world. Beyond the obvious and most important reason of keeping people safe, there are other indirect benefits of a sound safety program:

1. Preaching and practicing a safety aware culture boosts employee morale because it shows a caring and thoughtful attitude towards their well-being.

2. The client will feel more comfortable with a rigid safety structure because it directly carries over to their business's public perception and overall bottom line.

3. Management benefits because of less liability and worker compensation issues.

4. Productivity is steady because employees are on the job working instead of out due to preventable injuries.

5. Visitors and guests of your facility need to be assured of a healthy and safe environment. A positive experience leads to an improved public perception of trust in the brand.

Safety needs to be an intentional and integral part of your management plan. Live a safety minded lifestyle and you will begin to instill the safety minded culture in the workplace. Leading by example is the surest bet to creating a safety conscious paradigm shift.

Takeaway messages:

1. *Preach and practice safety, always.*

2. *Provide the training and equipment necessary. There is no reason to slack in this area.*

3. *Safety happens on purpose.*

4. *A sound safety culture offers indirect benefits and has positive impacts.*

12

Lessons Learned

Learning from mistakes builds wisdom. Consider the following quotes that perfectly summarize the importance of learning from our eventual mistakes and missteps.

The first is attributed to Socrates: *"Smart people learn from everything and everyone, average people learn from their experiences, and foolish people already have all the answers."*

The second is a quote from Nelson Mandela, *"I never lose. I either win or I learn."*

Experience is key in the world of facilities, but just as important is knowledge gained from other people's experiences. Lessons that are learned the hard way are not easily forgotten. Evaluate every crisis and failure immediately after the situation is resolved while everything is fresh in the memory. In the military, this type of debriefing is referred to as an after-action review and reinforces the importance of immediately reviewing the mission for successes and failures. Ask and answer the following three key questions and use as feedback for future improvement. Be critical and honest:

1. **What went wrong?** A list made of shortfalls soon after a failure form the basis of what solutions can be implemented to preclude future occurrences.

2. **What went well?** Don't just focus on the failures, but also highlight what went favorably. The reasons behind positive outcomes can always be strengthened and built upon. Realizing successes in the face of adversities is beneficial for the team's morale and motivation.

3. **What could be improved upon?** This means focus on the failures and the

near misses. These situations have major potential for improvements.

Everyone knows that shortcuts lead to bigger problems. There is an old tradesman's adage that preaches this, "The hard way is usually the easy way." Basically, doing things right initially, even though it may not seem the simplest method, usually ends up being the best way in the long term.

So why are "quick fixes" still practiced? We are all guilty of taking shortcuts in our lives—it is human nature. The remedy here is to make a consistent and conscious effort whenever a challenge arises; take a brief pause and think it through. Play the moves out like a chess game, scrutinizing all possible outcomes, consequences, and risks.

Sound facility management involves handling the immediate issue while simultaneously searching for ways to prevent or diminish the chances of the same problem from recurring. Run through the scenario and consider all available options, and ultimately choose the one that offers the long-term solution with the most favorable result.

Of course, this is certainly not always practical, but the point being that a few extra moments of deliberation and consideration taken in in the beginning will save time, frustration, and resources later.

Takeaway messages:

1. *Lessons learned are traditionally the best teachers. Use both your own experiences and the experiences of others to mitigate avoidable mistakes.*

2. *Conduct an after-action review following major events to take note of pluses and minuses.*

3. *Build upon what went well and fine-tune it, don't just focus on the failures.*

4. *Take a pause and think things through.*

5. *Sound facility management involves handling the immediate issue while simultaneously exploring ways to prevent or diminish the chances of the same problem from recurring.*

13

Summary of Takeaway Messages

- Become knowledgeable and well versed in a multitude of areas.

- If you do not know the answer, know how to find the answer.

- Stay curious and informed.

- Listen and understand the problem, then find an acceptable resolution.

- Remember, competence, consistency, and quality wins over customers at the end of the day.

- Learn early on what type of customers or clients you have and tailor your management style to fit them accordingly.

- Proactive communication is essential when problems are encountered.

- An exceptional employee will care about doing a good job. Everything matters to them and they pay attention to the details.

- An employee with initiative and integrity will always be a long-term asset to your organization.

- Once you find a high performing employee, do what it takes to keep them and grow them on your team.

- Avoid excessive turnover by creating a positive atmosphere that rewards success.

- Do not make the mistake of misjudging an employee's poor performance due to failure on your part to clearly communicate the mission.

- An inclusive, team-oriented workplace is vital for content employees.

- Empower employees by demonstrating they have a career progression path.

- Constantly stretch yourself and seek knowledge to grow and evolve.

- Do not procrastinate.

- Make effective use of time management strategies to maximize your own performance.

- Ensure seamless function--If you have managed, planned, and directed everything right, then operations should not fall apart when you're not present.

- Focus on the "why" of problems rather than the "who" of problems.

- Use grammatically correct, concise, and accurate replies.

- Know your audience when communicating.

- Take the time to fully comprehend what the client is communicating and then respond thoughtfully and appropriately.

- Lead by example and empathy.

- Lead with a clear, communicated vision.

- Do not let ego impede true leadership.

- Keep your promises to your client and your employees.

- Identify potential problem areas—both the obvious and not so obvious.

- Practice the emergency response periodically as a dry-run exercise.

- Maintain an adequate emergency equipment inventory. Perform routine preventative maintenance to ensure reliability.

- Practice safety always.

- Provide the training and equipment necessary. There is no reason to slack on safety.

- Safety happens on purpose.

- Lessons learned are traditionally the best teachers. Use both your own experiences and the experiences of others to mitigate avoidable mistakes.

- Take time to pause and think things through.

- Eliminate causes of unnecessary workplace stress

- A smoothly functioning organization involves team building and an open feedback loop

- Build upon what went well and fine-tune it, don't just focus on the failures.

- Sound facility management involves handling the immediate issue while simultaneously searching for ways to prevent the same problem from recurring.

- It can be beneficial to surround yourself with people who do not always agree with your ideas so differing perspectives can be offered.

- Conduct an after-action review following major events to take note of pluses and minuses.

- Encourage building off the small wins to cultivate even greater successes.

- Leverage informal communication opportunities that can provide benefit for the entire team.

- A good first step in communication is confirming that the entire organization is on the same page with the end results in mind.

www.ingramcontent.com/pod-product-compliance
Lightning Source LLC
Chambersburg PA
CBHW052330220526
45472CB00001B/350